Stuck in the mud

Help! Help!

"Help, help! Please help.
I'm stuck. I'm stuck in the
mud," puffed the old man.

"I slipped on the wet mud," puffed the old man.

"Quick, get a rope," said Pen.

"The old man is wet and cold,"
said Pen. "We must get him up."

"Quick, we must help him,"
said Pen.

"Get it," said Rob.
"Get hold of it!" he said.

"Hold it," yelled Pen.
"Hold the rope!"

"Let's fix it on the trunk,"
said Rob.

"Spot, get help," said Pen.
"Quick, get help.
Get the men.
Get the men to help us."

Spot ran and ran.

"Hold the rope," said Pen.

Up, up,
up…

Down, down he slid!
"We *must* get him up,"
said Rob. "We must!"

"Hold the rope," said Pen.

Up, up, up.

"He will be OK!" said the men.
"The old man will be OK."
Pen and Rob felt very pleased.